Welcome Home,

By: Shani Riviere

Welcome Home, Little One!

By: Shani Riviere

www.shanithedoula.com

Welcome Home, Little One!

The day had come, so big and bright, A day so special, filled with light!

Mommy and Daddy held hands so tight,

Waiting to hold you, our hearts took flight.

We heard your voice, so soft and new, A tiny giggle, a cry or two. Our hearts grew bigger, love so true, Oh, little one, we welcomed you!

Wrapped in a blanket,
snug and warm,
We promised to keep
you safe
from harm.
Your tiny fingers,
your tiny toes,
Oh, how our love for
you just grows!

Through the doors and out
we go, Into the world,
where love will show.
The car ride home, so calm,
so sweet,
A brand-new journey, oh
what a treat!

Into your room, so soft and bright,
Your cozy bed tucked in just right.
Toys and blankets, books galore, A home for you forevermore.

Rocking gently, side to side,
Holding you close, with love and pride.
Whispers, kisses, soft lullabies,
Sweet dreams dance in sleepy eyes.

As days go by, we laugh, we play,
We watch you grow in every way.
Cuddles, giggles, songs so true, Every moment, loving you.

Welcome home, our little star,
No matter what, just as you are.
With love so big, so wild, so free,
You'll always belong with
Daddy and me!

"As you take your first breaths in this world, know that you are deeply loved and cherished. Welcome home, little one—your journey has just begun, and the world is brighter because you are here."

Welcome
Home
Little One!

The New Begininning

Made in the USA
Columbia, SC
21 April 2025

56623123R00015